Serendipity Of A Clumsy Heart

Love conquers all

Azula

BookLeaf
Publishing

India | USA | UK

Made with ❤ on the BookLeaf Publishing Platform

www.bookleafpub.in

www.bookleafpub.com

Dedication

For the hearts that beat off-rhythm,
for the lovers who trip over their own feet,
and for the souls who have ever looked at their own
beautiful mess
and found a universe smiling back.
This is for you.

Preface

These poems are not perfect. They are born from a commitment to honour the heart in all its clumsy glory. This collection is a diary of stumbles, surprises, and the quiet serendipity found in simply trying. They are snapshots of messy feelings and fleeting thoughts. May you find a reflection of your own beautiful journey within these pages.

Acknowledgements

To the catalyst: For the unexpected spark that set this all in motion. You were the beautiful accident, the unanswered question, the gentle chaos that my poetry needed. Thank you for being the serendipity.

To my anchors: My family and friends, who have always provided the softest places to land. Thank you for celebrating my awkwardness, for listening to half-formed verses at midnight, and for reminding me that a clumsy step is still a step forward. Your unwavering belief is the steady ground beneath my feet.

And finally, to you, the reader: Thank you. For picking up this collection, you have agreed to hold a piece of my heart in your hands. My deepest hope is that it feels familiar, that it offers solace, and that it reminds you of the quiet, resilient magic brewing within your own chest. This journey is only complete now that it has found its way to you.

With immense gratitude,

1. Storm and Silence

She lived in lines, in quiet grace,
A perfect mask, a polished face.
Then came the storm — wild, loud, and free,
A spark that stirred the still in her.
He broke the rules,
Laughed in the hush of silent halls.
She hated him — or so she said,
But envied all the life he led.
One word too far — She made him fall,
Restored the calm, erased it all.
In that moment silence lingered, soft and wide,
And something in her sighed, not cried.
She won the fight,
Yet missed the warmth behind his mischief.
And deep within, a quiet flame
Whispers: She, too, can learn to change.

2. Shadows and Sparks

The ice had thawed — she missed the storm,
His teasing now a daily norm.
But then a girl with warmth and grace
Lit up the room and shared the space.
They laughed, they talked,
While she watched from her quiet chair.
Left out, unseen, she felt the sting,
A silent ache that words don't bring.
Yet every time he turned to tease,
It soothed her heart, a gentle breeze.
She learned that even mischief's art
Could hold a place within the heart.
From ashes of jealousy, she would grow,
for in light and shadow, their bond would show.
A twist in the tale, a lesson in disguise,
in the warmth of connection, a solace would rise in the
future unseen.

3. Unseen Threads

She counted days just to say "hi,"
Weekends stretched like endless sky.
His laugh, his glance — her daily sun,
Until one day, everything changed.
His seat moved on, the space grew cold,
Their story paused, or so she told.
She walked alone, her smile thin,
A quiet ache beneath her skin.
She passed a house, the same old street,
A teasing call would meet her ear —
Too soft to name, yet strangely clear.
She never guessed, not then, not quite,
That he still watched her out of sight.
Though space had grown, one truth remained:
She'd never truly left his frame.
As if the universe conspired to weave their paths,
waiting for the day when time would bend,
and laughter would bridge the space between them
again.

4. Curtain Fall

The year-end feast, a blur of light,
With laughter echoing through the night.
They'd grown too far, no words remained,
Just fleeting thoughts, she never named.
She saw him now like passing rain —
A glance, a stir, then gone again.
Her heart would lift, then quickly fall,
A whisper lost in crowded halls.
Then came the play — a solemn scene,
He played a soul whose time would part.
And as he fell, her breath grew tight,
The stage dissolved in blinding white.
A weight she'd never known took hold,
A sorrow sudden, sharp, and bold.
And in that hush, her spirit stirred —
A chasm of longing opened, echoing within her,
A feeling deeper than a word could express.

5. Golden Haze

She loved the summer's golden haze —
The tropical fruit scent, the sunlit days.
Yet now and then, her thoughts would stray,
To wonder how he spent his day.
One quiet morning, beneath the sun,
She spoke to plants, her daily fun.
Then — like a dream not meant to stay —
He wandered past, just feet away.
A moment swift, a twist of fate.
Her body moved before her mind,
She ducked and hid, her breath confined.
Why was he there? Her heartbeat wild,
A question sharp, a thought beguiled.
But fate had played a gentle trick —
A glance, a path, a moment quick.
He'd seen her street, her world, her place,
And now he passed to glimpse her face.

6. The Request

Each chasing dreams through shifting gears.
She hoped to find him once again,
In lecture halls or campus rain.
But fate had drawn a different line —
Another city, another time.
She let the feeling fade away,
Amused it ever held such sway.
Then one warm noon, with laughter light,
She walked beneath the sun's soft bite.
A face appeared — a distant flame,
Her breath caught still, he looked the same.
A glance half-held, too shy to bear,
He saw her then, but silence stayed,
The moment stretched, then softly frayed.
Like threads of light through shifting air.
And later still, when days grew cold,
when she joined the world where stories unfold.
A friend request — his name, his face,
As if he'd waited for that space.

7. Whisper of a click

Her heart, a quiet garden,
swayed with a breeze unseen—
a name appeared like a whisper
soft as dusk on her screen.
She wore nonchalance like perfume,
but within,
a thousand lanterns lit.
The profile she made just to find him.
A picture, her real name—just in case.
But before she could search,
he found her.
A request.
A breath held.
Above the clouds, she clicked *accept.*
Then came the message:
"Hi."
Years of silence,
now a single word opened a door
she thought was forever closed.

8. A Contradiction

She wandered into his world,
a quiet guest,
where words could finally bloom—
but misted doubt
clouded her thoughts.
Was this feeling hers alone?
So she cloaked her truth
in gentle laughter,
called him *friend*,
while her soul
had already named him more.
He, timeless in his teasing,
stirred echoes of past—
moments that shimmered
like sunlight on old corridors.
She waited for his words
as night waits for dawn—
brief, golden,
enough to feel alive again.
Then came the question:

"Do you have a boyfriend?"
She smiled,
"A boy, and a friend—that's you."
Another veil,
another dance around the flame.
He searched her silence
like a poet reads between lines,
but she spoke in riddles,
while her heart
had already chosen him.

9. No moon

She spoke in half-moons and shadows,
never quite whole, never quite gone.
He asked.
She paused.
He reached.
She rose —
but only to build another wall.
Her heart was loud,
but her lips were quiet.
Texts turned to echoes,
"Hi" and "Bye" like passing trains.
She held her love like sand—
tight, trembling—
until it slipped through,
grain by grain,
Then one day,
she whispered his name.
Not loud.
Not bold.
And the wall?

It didn't fall.
It listened.
And something —
something began to grow, or so she thought.

10. Who is she?

The signs were there.
The drift was quiet,
but clear.
He spoke of choices—
not her.
She ignored the signs
like she ignored her own heart.
She thought love couldn't fade.
She thought he'd stay.
But he grew tired
of waiting at a door
that never opened.
So he posted it—
two pair of shoes,
one sunset,
a message without words.
He hoped it would wake her.
But it broke her instead.
She drowned in silence,
and tears,

when morning came,

she whispered:

"I let him go long before he left."

She changed.

Not for revenge.

Not for him.

For her.

Piece by piece,

she rebuilt the girl she buried

But he?

He spoke her name

to the girl beside him.

Over

And again.

The other girl,

tired of being second

to a ghost he couldn't let go,

knew she was never the one.

11. Ghost lines

They thought they were stars in different skies,
She changed in hush, he longed with sighs.
He reached again, heart on his sleeve,
But she believed his love wasn't hers to claim.
A meeting set, a fragile thread,
She failed to meet, stayed home instead.
No word was sent, he stood alone,
His heart turned cold, his temper grown.
He wrote in rage, his sorrow bold.
Words like thorns, too sharp, too fast—
And just like that, the moment passed.
She vanished then, a ghost in time,
Six months lost in silent rhyme.
He searched for ways to make it right,
But found no path, no guiding light.
Then through a friend, he found the thread,
"Call her yourself," the message read.

12. Dilemma

He held the key, yet lingered still,
A breath between the want and will.
The number glowed, the silence grew—
Would she still care?
Each ring a ripple through his chest,
A storm beneath a calm unrest.
His mind withdrew, his heart held fast,
To echoes of a love long past.
Then—soft as dusk—the line came live,
A single word, a voice revived.

Hello.

No rush, no cry, no flame—
Just silence, trembling, saying names.
Two souls suspended, caught in air,
Not lost, not found—just simply there.

13. Just this once

A dream still fresh, a name still near,
She stared at the screen, gripped by fear.
A call she never thought would come,
From lips once silent, now undone.
She hesitated—heart in war,
Between the ache and what's in store.
Just this once, she told the night,
And answered fate with quiet might.
"Hello," she breathed, the line went still,
Two souls suspended by sheer will.
He asked, "How are you?"—soft, unsure,
She answered not with hope or fear,
But with a heart that longed to hear.
They spoke of time, of wounds and grace,
Of moments lost they couldn't trace.
Then bold as fire, her voice took flight:
"What are your goals? Is this our fight?
Why now? this call? What do you see?
Would you... would you marry me?"
He froze, the world began to spin—

Could love return from deep within?
Then through the storm, his voice broke free:
"Yes," he said, "If you'll have me."

14. Cupcake

She held the answers, yet her heart whispered doubt.
On her birthday, he brought no grandeur—A cupcake, a
candle, and a smile.
"Make a wish," he said.
And in that flicker of flame, she knew—
The feelings were deep, and true.
Words failed, but their silence spoke volumes.
Time blinked, the meeting ended,
Yet the memory lingered longer than the moment.
Love had bloomed.
In stolen glances, shared meals,
In laughter that felt like déjà vu.
Their love was not a story,
but a symbol—
a candle that burned in two worlds,
never consumed,
always glowing.

15. Predicament

Through storms and stillness, they held fast—
two stars chasing separate skies.
Dreams called her beyond borders,
and he, though aching, became her wind.
At the terminal of fate,
they mistook time for kindness.
Two gates—one to the world, one to home—
divided by architecture, not intention.
He ran, heart pounding like a drum in a void,
bargaining with stone-faced sentinels.
But destiny had already closed its door.
There she stood,
behind a glass that shimmered like frozen time.
So close,
yet sealed in a silence no touch could break.
His tears fell like broken constellations,
his knees gave way to the weight of absence.
She watched,
a ghost in motion,
her own heart fracturing like stained glass.

They were two suns,
caught in eclipse—
light yearning for light,
but never touching.

16. Yearning

Though galaxies now lay between them,
their hearts remained in orbit—
two celestial bodies,
forever drawn by unseen gravity.
She wandered foreign skies,
chasing constellations of ambition.
He stayed grounded,
a lighthouse in her memory,
sending light through the void.
They wrote—
not with ink,
but with stardust and longing.
Each letter a comet,
burning across the silence,
carrying fragments of soul.
At night,
he dreamed of her in surreal landscapes—
a train made of moonlight,
a garden blooming with forgotten words.
She appeared always just beyond reach,

smiling like a secret.
She too dreamed—
of him waiting beneath a sky
where stars whispered their names.
Even oceans of time
couldn't drown the echo.
Their love became myth—
a story told by the wind,
a rhythm felt in the pulse of the universe.
Though apart,
they were never truly alone.
They were twin stars,
writing verses in the dark,
waiting for the day
their orbits would align once more.

17. POV

Her dreams whispered her back home,
where new doors opened with familiar warmth.
A reunion wrapped in hope.
But love, once effortless,
now stumbled over words unspoken.

Her thoughts:

Don't we deserve the peace of certainty?
I've waited long enough—
I need to know we're building something real."

His thoughts:

"I love her, truly.
But why does it feel like pressure now?
Can't love breathe without being boxed in?
Their hearts beat for each other,
but their minds danced in different rhythms.
Each argument carved silence,
each silence echoed doubt.
Love was still there—
but so was the storm.

18. Lost cause

Despite clashing dreams,
they chose courage—
to speak, to hope, to face the storm.
She trembled before her parents,
the perfect daughter's mask cracking.
Tears fell with truth:
"If not him, then no one."
Her father softened,
a meeting was set.
Questions flew like arrows—He stood tall,
his heart louder than doubt.
But just as light peeked through,
Cultural walls rose high,
and love was left outside.
He whispered:
"She is the one I want."
But both families turned away.
Two hearts, once full,
now shattered in silence.
It felt like the end—

but love rarely fades so easily.

19. Vows

When the world turned quiet,
they sat with the silence—
not broken, just waiting.
A letter arrived,
a path to distant lands.
His dream, her ache.
She said it would be fine.
But as the days thinned,
the air between them grew still,
heavy with unspoken fear.
He chose not to wait.
"Let's marry before I leave,"
spoken gently,
like a promise to the wind.
She asked,
and after long hours and longer silences,
her parents, though unsure,
chose her quiet joy.
No crowd, no celebration—
just two hands,

wrapped in simple vows.

and a moment that felt like home.

His family remained in shadow,

but his heart stood in light.

Then came the parting.

She wept softly,

as night folded around her.

And though distance stretched between them once more,

they remained—

not untouched,

but unwavering.

20. 4394 miles

He left with the wind,
and she stayed with the silence.
No farewells loud,
just a quiet ache shared between two hearts.
Letters became lifelines,
calls—soft bridges across time zones.
They spoke not of longing,
but of little things—
a meal, a memory, a moment.
The world moved on,
but they remained—
threaded together by something deeper than presence.
Back home, whispers stirred.
A glance too tender,
a word too careful.
Truth, once buried,
began to rise like mist.
They didn't rush it.
Love had taught them patience.
And somewhere between distance and discovery,

they found a rhythm—
not loud,
but lasting.

21. End & Beginning

Life, in its restless rhythm,
pulled them apart more than once—
but each time,
they returned,
not as they were,
but stronger, softer, more sure.
He came back,
not to rewrite the past,
but to hold the present with both hands.
This time, he didn't whisper—
he stood in the light,
and chose her.
His words,
simple and steady,
found their way to hearts
that had once hesitated.
And slowly,
like morning mist lifting,
acceptance bloomed.
No grand stage,

just a quiet garden,
a few chairs,
and the scent of belonging.
They looked at each other—
not with longing,
but with knowing.
Their vows were not loud,
but they echoed deep.
Through every storm,
every silence,
they had stayed.
And in the clumsy beauty of life,
they found their serendipity—
not perfect,
but true.
Love, after all,
isn't about never falling apart.
It's about always finding your way back.

www.ingramcontent.com/pod-product-compliance
Lightning Source LLC
Chambersburg PA
CBHW050959030426
42339CB00007B/406